RIGHT WAYS OF RAISING TEEN: Positive Parenting Tips and Understanding Teen for Better Communication

Sharon C. Roll

Table of contents

Chapter 1

Teens feelings

Mood swings, or emotional ups and downs, are a typical and significant aspect of teenage development. Adolescence is a time of significant transition, and thus, teenagers experience a wide range of powerful and shifting emotions. By talking, listening, and maintaining contact, you may assist teens in coping with emotional ups and downs.

When moods affect daily functioning, this can indicate a more serious mental health issue. Consult your child and your doctor if you have concerns about your child. relating to teen moods Young individuals, like adults, experience moods or emotional ups and downs on a regular basis.

It's common for teens to feel happy and enthusiastic on some days and sad, flat, or depressed on others.

In other instances, Teenagers frequently need more solitude or alone time, which is completely acceptable. These emotional ups and downs might occur more frequently and to a greater degree throughout the adolescent years.

Physical, emotional, social, and psychological factors can all play a role in your child's emotional ups and downs; no single factor alone is to blame. Frequently, neither you nor your kid will be able to pinpoint the exact cause of how they are feeling.

Moods are an indication that your child is dealing with more complicated adult emotions and is making an effort to comprehend and regulate them. This is a critical stage in adolescent development. You have a significant responsibility to assist your child with this section.

Why do emotional ups and downs occur? physical elements Adolescence is a time of significant bodily change for young individuals.

They may feel self-conscious or uncomfortable about their changing bodies, or they may just desire more time and space to themselves. Children who appear to be maturing sooner or later than their peers might have emotional reactions to these physical changes.

The amount of sleep your youngster needs is another physical aspect. Teenagers require 8 to 10 hours of sleep every night, and how much sleep they receive might have an impact on their mood.

Your child's physical health will benefit from regular, wholesome meals and adequate exercise, which may also aid with emotional ups and downs.

mental aspects The teenage years bring about a lot of changes in the brain.

For instance, your child's body produces sex hormones as a result of brain changes. These hormones cause bodily changes as well as feelings of sex and romance. For your child, these brand-new emotions can be intense and perhaps perplexing.
Your child's brain will continue to develop until they are in their early 20s. The prefrontal cortex, the final portion of the brain to mature, is intimately linked to the regions in charge of regulating and managing emotions.

This implies that your child could struggle to restrain some of their more intense feelings, and it might appear that they respond more emotionally to circumstances than they did in the past. They are still figuring out how to handle and communicate their emotions in a mature manner.

emotional and social influences. Your child's mood might be affected by new ideas, feelings, acquaintances, and obligations. As they progress toward independence, your kid is learning how to deal with more challenges on their own. Additionally, your child is spending more time in their own heads than they used to and is preoccupied with problems like friendships, school, and family ties.

Your child's mood might also be affected by stressful familial events.
assisting teens to have more ups than downs
There are a few things you can do to support your child in experiencing more highs than lows.
The first step is to identify what your youngster already finds enjoyable. Some examples of these include engaging in a favorite sport, hanging out with old friends, enjoying music or making it, painting,

making their own digital material, and so on. Maintaining these activities will provide your child a sense of stability and grounding and give them a foundation from which to explore new interests.
You may assist your child in discovering new pursuits that will test them, enable them to establish new objectives, and allow them to make new friends. These can include taking up a new hobby or joining a different social group. Instead of selecting these activities for your child, you may try listening to what they say about what they enjoy and hate to glean hints about potential new interests.

Assisting young people with emotional ups and downs Your youngster will inevitably experience low or depressed moods. To assist your child with the ups and downs, you may take a variety of actions.
Assisting your child in dealing with ups and downsYour youngster may benefit greatly from understanding that emotional ups and

downs are common. One of the best ways to accomplish this is to let your child know that you have flat spots from time to time. Additionally, it's crucial for your child to know that you'll be there for them if they're struggling or feeling down. Simply stating, "I can tell you're having a terrible day," might be helpful.

Keeping in contact with your child
You'll be able to identify the reasons for your child's emotional ups and downs more readily if you stay in touch with them and pay attention to what's happening in their lives. The ideal moments for your child to share things with you might sometimes be during routine, everyday activities like taking them someplace or watching TV together.
allowing your youngster some roomYouth are becoming more independent and taking on new challenges. Try to allow your youngster time or space to reflect on fresh feelings and experiences while they're doing

this. Make sure your youngster knows you are available if they need to chat.

withholding solutions If there is a problem, it might be nice to talk about solutions with your child, but they must be ones that they contributed to and feel like they "own." If your child believes they contributed to the solution, they are more inclined to attempt it.
Another important life skill that your child will develop through practice is problem-solving. You may demonstrate that you appreciate your child's involvement in decisions that will have an impact on their lives by investing time and effort into helping them improve their problem-solving abilities.

collaborating to develop coping mechanisms. One of the major tasks of adolescence is learning to deal with and regulate emotional ups and downs on one's own. And you can assist your child in learning this critical life skill.

Making a list of "mood busters" with your child is one method to do this. Your youngster can do these actions to feel better. For instance,

Your youngster should have a few choices on the list so they may experiment and choose what works best.

Being an example Your child still looks to you as their primary role model. Your child will watch you to see how you handle difficult situations. Consider how your child would see you employing coping mechanisms and problem-solving techniques.

More than just moods, when teens are constantly depressed Constantly feeling gloomy or uninspired might occasionally be an indication of something more serious. Young individuals may have depressive symptoms for a short period of time, or for several days or more. If your kid exhibits depressive, flat, irritable, or sad behaviors for two weeks or more, or if you observe that their emotions prevent them from engaging in their regular daily activities, this may indicate a more significant mental health issue.

It's crucial to chat with your child and seek expert assistance if you have concerns about their feelings or behavior. Your general doctor (GP) can direct you to the appropriate source.

When teens with mental health issues receive treatment, especially early therapy, the majority of them recover successfully.

Chapter 2

Listening to your teens

How to inspire your teen to open up to you by genuinely listening to them. When we questioned a group of children between the ages of 13 and 17, they expressed a desire to be able to connect with their parents in healthy, constructive ways.
Are you serious? As much as you want to connect with your teenager, he does too! Children want to speak with us!
Where is the breakdown then?

Some children only require an invitation. Some people require more time to open up. Yet some people, like the young woman who claimed, "Every time I try to communicate with my parents, they either shout at me before I finish my complete tale or scold me," are more passive. I would speak with them a lot more if they were more receptive

to talking to me and allowed me to say more things.
Things can improve no matter where you and your teen are on the speaking continuum. And they will if you utilize some of the methods that concerned parents, youth workers, and counselors have been employing with their charges. Let's fill your toolkit for communication so that you and your adolescent may connect on a deeper level.

Listening Devices Here are seven strategies to ensure that you are truly listening to your teenager and that they are aware of it.
1.Pay him your undivided attention. I am aware of how busy you are and how little time you have for yourself. But multitasking is not appropriate at this moment. Whatever is vying for your attention, such as the TV, lawnmower, or mixer, has to be turned off.
2. Instead of mocking her feelings, consider them.Teenagers adore catching a glimpse of their emotions on your face. It conveys to

them that you are aware of their feelings about today's coach's yelling. Remember that their universe is smaller than yours, which makes each occurrence appear larger, especially if their feelings or the causes behind them seem exaggerated or frivolous.

3. Describe what he said in your own words. Consider that your son is seeing Jen. He tells you about Jen flirting with his closest buddy when he gets home one day. So, from what I understand you to say, it truly stung when Jen gave Brian the look she usually gives you when she stared at Brian. Restating your response makes sure you're hearing your adolescent clearly. Your kid has the opportunity to explain again if you accurately rephrase the scenario.

4. Display an alert demeanor. Avoid sighing, rolling of the eyes, crossing of the arms, and glancing over your shoulder or into the distance. Cross your legs and sit on the floor, a couch, or the back of a chair with

your arms at your sides. Lean slightly forward and nod as necessary.

5. Make the choice to pay attention to what she has to say. Coming home to a teenager who wants to talk about topics that seem trivial to you might be difficult after a long day at work. To make yourself desire to listen, pray to God. You'll become more interested in her life as you listen carefully and clarify your queries. It could be beneficial to remind yourself that she is the object of your true interest.

6. Pay attention to behavior.How do you go about that? If your kid is slamming doors or leaving suspicious letters from a boyfriend or girlfriend lying around the house, you will notice. Is there a problem at school? Are you linked up?

7. Watch for opportunities to be open and vulnerable. Teenagers occasionally lose it and express what's on their minds. Give them as much time as necessary to share

when they do so. Then inquire, "Do you want me to offer advice or assistance? Or would you rather I simply listen?

Location Resources It is important how you communicate with your adolescent.Consternation against communication may result from it. The following four considerations should be made for the locations where you speak:

1. Choose a location that offers an "out." If there is something else to talk about when things get uncomfortable, kids believe it is easier to talk to their parents. Examples of "safety valves" include driving, eating, playing games, going for walks in the park, putting together puzzles, drawing, visiting museums, and riding bikes. Teenagers want to converse, but they don't want the strain of having to do so nonstop.

2. Avoid becoming distracted. A safety valve (see #1) provides comfort; a distraction, whether you want it to or not, draws attention. Is there a nice area to converse in

that restaurant, or is the music constantly too loud? Do you have your pager off? Will you be able to hear your little brother hitting the tennis ball against the garage door if you are talking in the living room? Even in-car chats with one teen's parents were ineffective: "Sometimes [my parents] are too focused on driving or whatever they are doing and don't pay attention to what I am saying."

3.Pick a secure location. Children seek a setting where they may open up about the difficult aspects of their hearts. Where is it for your adolescents? his bedroom? With yours? on a running trail? Ask if you don't know; it's acceptable.

4. If you locate a location that functions, persist with it. Consider bringing your teen out for lunch or breakfast once a week. Create a routine like this, and your children may feel at ease enough to open up and even pose challenging life issues. However, try to

refrain from bringing your own list of challenging questions; if they develop interrogations or preaching sessions, your adolescent may start to avoid such mealtimes.

Chapter 3

Talking and staying connected to your teens

Sustaining healthy connections and relationships Parents and kids frequently start to spend more time apart during adolescence. Teenagers' desire to spend time alone as well as with friends and others outside of their homes is understandable.

To feel safe and secure while they navigate the trials of puberty, however, teens still require their parents' close bonds. Your kid will feel more confident attempting new things and exploring new ideas, interests, and relationships when they know you are there to love and support them.
Maintaining contact with your adolescent child involves strengthening your bond with them by being accessible and accommodating to their needs. It involves more than just being in the same vicinity.

You can connect by:
Casual dating is when you develop intimacy through regular encounters; scheduled dating is when you set aside time to do activities you both like. Having two kinds of connection in your relationship with your child is fantastic.
You'll be better able to identify any issues your child may be facing if you maintain contact with them. Additionally, your

youngster is more likely to approach you with issues.

Teenagers are better prepared to gain independence and mature into responsible adults when they have solid, loving, trustworthy, and open connections with their parents. Additionally, they have a higher likelihood of handling dangerous circumstances well, such as smoking, drinking, using other drugs, and engaging in sexual behavior.

I casually interact with teens and preteens. Using commonplace interactions to establish enduring connections is known as "casual connecting. The best chances for informal interaction arise when your child initiates conversation with you, because this usually indicates that they are in the mood to chat.

Advice for informal interaction

Put an end to what you're doing and concentrate on the now. Put away your phone, for instance, or turn off your computer. Give your youngster your undivided attention, even if it's just for a little while. The greatest way to establish a connection is to convey that your child is your top priority right now. While your child is speaking to you, pay attention to them. Pay close attention to what they have to say. This communicates to your youngster that you value their opinions and display enthusiasm. Encourage your kid to elaborate on what they've said and to talk about their ideas, feelings, and aspirations or future goals without interjecting, opining, or correcting. Unless they specifically want it, your goal should be to just be there with your child. Just show up. Like when your child is studying at the table and you are in the kitchen. Teenagers gain from simply being aware of your availability. Maintain contact. For instance, if you don't live with your child full-time or you're gone from home for a long time, send daily texts.

Additionally, you might actively work to generate chances for informal interactions. For instance, some teens find it easier to converse while you two are engaged in a shared activity like cooking, walking, or cleaning. But if your kid is reluctant to chat, don't press the issue. Simply wait for a different chance.
It was planned to engage with preteens and teenagers. Planned interaction demonstrates to your child that you value your time together.

The ability to have fun together might be hampered by busy schedules and increased separation time. You must therefore plan it. Even though teenagers don't always like spending time with their parents, it's important to urge that they do it sometimes. suggestions for planned connectivity.
Plan to spend time together. You must choose a time that works for both of you. Initially, keeping the duration short might be beneficial. Follow your child's lead and

let them decide what you'll do. Your youngster will be inspired to want to spend time with you as a result. It's entertaining to attempt things where your child is the expert; having your child teach you a new ability might help them feel more confident. Keep your attention on taking in your child's companionship. Make an effort to actively participate in what your child is doing and to be an enthusiastic participant. The conversation and shared enjoyment with your child are more significant than the action itself. Instead of scolding or advising your youngster, show curiosity and acceptance.

Although giving up your job as a teacher and coach is difficult, this is the perfect moment to develop and strengthen your bond. Therefore, if you spot a mistake or a simpler way to do a task, just let it alone. Try again and be optimistic. Your youngster might not be as eager to participate in these activities at first as you are. Your youngster will grow to love this time with you if you keep scheduled times to a minimum at first. By removing barriers to connection, Your child refuses to interact with you. You may overcome this obstacle by making the most of regular opportunities to interact, such as talking on the phone while driving.

You might attempt the following if your kid is unwilling to spend time with you:
Keep it brief at first. For instance, after school, try getting a cup of coffee at your preferred café. Find impromptu methods to spend time with loved ones rather than making plans in advance. Ask your child to make a list of activities they would like to do with you, then go through the items on the list. Technology may be used to communicate with your youngster. Staying in touch may be made easier by sending amusing texts or memes. Never give up. Although it could take some time, the more time you spend together, the more at ease you'll both feel. Your youngster won't discuss their activities with you.

If you take advantage of informal talks throughout the day, you and your child could feel more connected. Every small conversation is an opportunity to listen and speak in a laid-back, uplifting manner.
You believe that you are the only one trying. When you treat your child with kindness and consideration, this can foster goodwill and positive emotions. Saying please, offering hugs, pats on the back, knocking before entering a bedroom, making a favorite meal, or organizing unexpected and enjoyable events are just a few examples of small things that may go a long way.

Even if your youngster isn't participating, this strategy fosters a more positive environment. Even when you don't feel like it, try to be kind to others. This gives your kid an excellent example and makes them appreciate the importance of spending time with you.

Additionally, when you feel like you are the only one working, try to keep in mind that this stage generally passes.

Chapter 4

Know when your teens are triggered

Making Your Teen Aware of Warning Signs and Triggers It is normal to occasionally feel perplexed by your teen's conduct because raising teenagers is no easy task. Your teen could act out over anything at first glance. However, the circumstances—often referred to as "triggers"—that tend to push your teen's buttons might have patterns. An occurrence, a sensation, or a circumstance that precedes an emotional response is referred to as a "trigger." The key to halting the out of control conduct is to assist your kid in becoming more aware of those triggers. The following actions can help your teen become more aware:

Keep an eye out for patterns in your teen's conduct. We frequently talk about a trigger as a prelude to an irrational outburst, but triggers may also be a prelude to a variety of reactions. The following are examples of events and emotions that may "press your teen's buttons" and cause an outburst: receiving a "no" is awful news. being excluded, abused, or criticized Ignorance Ignorance of what to doOverstimulation Of course, just as each adolescent is unique, so too will your teen's triggers be.
Observing and being familiar with the circumstances that cause your child to get agitated, annoyed, or unhappy is the first step in assisting your adolescent in becoming aware of triggers. Look for patterns and connections while keeping an eye out for trigger warning indications.

Think in reverse. If your teen does have an outburst, go back to what led up to it. When it's time for them to prepare for a test, for instance, your kid can become irate and restless. This may be a trigger; perhaps your youngster is having trouble in class and is having second thoughts about his academic prowess. Anxiety over receiving a poor mark or a sense of inadequacy might act as the catalyst.
Take into account your teen's viewpoint. Even while you might think you know what happened, your child might have had a different perspective. After giving your kid some time to collect themselves, ask them to describe what happened after everything has calmed down. Sincere listening to how your adolescent describes what happened might provide crucial information about triggers.

Initially, the discussion Triggers and feelings are closely related. The issue is how your kid perceives and interprets the trigger, not the trigger itself. So that you can both speak honestly and openly, pick a moment when you and your teen are both calm and relaxed, not in the midst of an outburst. Inform your teen of your findings regarding their triggers and associated behaviors.For instance, you may say, "I've seen that you lose your temper and become irritated when you're preparing for a test." Ask your teen about their feelings before, during, and after the incident. Give your teen wide rein to explore. The topic of trigger awareness is brought up in this conversation.

Be persistent. Finally, let your kid know that you are available as a resource. You are your teen's strongest supporter and the foundation of their network. Triggers might change as life changes. Finding and controlling triggers can be difficult, but assisting your teen in becoming aware of their own triggers can be a game-changer for your family. Your kid can eventually learn to recognize their triggers and create a strategy for a constructive reaction.

Chapter 5

Controlling teens emotions

Although it is often challenging, raising teens can be highly rewarding. Your child may be cheerful and talkative one minute, but then, all of a sudden, doors may slam and you may start to get the cold shoulder. Things that you might consider to be little inconveniences can seem like enormous problems to an adolescent.
Unfortunately, parents of middle and high school students are sometimes unaware of

the events that caused their teen distress.Have they received a low score on a test? Do they fear being accepted to college? Did a friend's Instagram image depict the enjoyment of everyone else? Do they experience bullying?

The good news is that you can support your kid in controlling their emotions even if you're unsure of what's wrong. Here are nine suggestions for comprehending your teen's emotions and supporting them through difficult times. storms.

1. Keep your cool. Avoid talking to your teen while you're upset, worn out, or irritable whenever you can. If you and your teenager get into a heated fight, maintaining your composure might help settle things down. It might be hard to remain calm when a teenager is yelling at you or banging on doors. Keep in mind that your objective is to help your child deal with his or her current

emotions and, over time, develop into an emotionally stable adult, not to win an argument. That doesn't mean you have to grin and nod when you're called names. But refrain from adding to the commotion by screaming yourself. Instead, explain to your youngster that it will be simpler to solve the issue at hand.If you can respect one another despite your differences,

2. Recognize the adolescent brainThe teenage brain is not as developed as the adult brain, despite the fact that teens can appear to be adults physically. Up until the mid-20s, the area of the brain that controls emotions, reason, and decision-making continued to develop. Your teen's thoughts and behaviors may alter as a result of both ongoing brain growth and hormonal changes that occur throughout these years. There is in no way a deficit of intelligence throughout the adolescent years as a result of these hormonal changes. Teenagers may struggle with resolving disagreements,

making wise decisions, and controlling their emotions since their self-management abilities are still developing.

3. Even while your attempts to engage your kid in discussion won't always be successful, it's crucial to make yourself available. Ask your adolescent to reciprocate by maintaining eye contact with you while you speak and listen to them. Consider mandating that technology (such as phones or televisions) be avoided during mealtimes, even if it means eating in silence.Find areas of agreement and talk about shared interests. If you are available during the good times, your adolescent is more likely to turn to you during the difficult times.

4.Gnaw on your tongue. Try to maintain an impartial stance if you're fortunate enough to have a teen open up to you about what's hurting them. Don't immediately pass judgment, for instance, if you believe your child was at fault in a dispute with a buddy at school. Well, I don't blame him for being furious; it seems like you were being a jerk," Give noncommittal comments to demonstrate that you are listening instead, and give your kid room and time to resolve the problem on their own. If you do reply, it may be beneficial to rephrase any unfavorable or ineffective beliefs. Always keep in mind that even though your adolescent is discussing an issue, It's not always that he or she wants you to repair it. Teens (and adults) frequently want want to express their problems without being inundated with answers.

5. Respect Their Divergent Points of View
You can imagine how you would feel if your partner informed you during a heated dispute that your worries were "not that big of an issue." Teenagers also don't want their

feelings to be downplayed. They frequently experience worry at this stage of their lives over life beyond high school or they may experience self-consciousness due to their changing bodies and emotions. This may cause even little issues to seem overwhelming to them. It also helps to be aware that your kid can genuinely believe that a tiny occurrence is the end of the world, even if you don't necessarily think that it is.

6. Offer Outlets Instead of allowing those difficult teen emotions to fester and burst, you may assist your adolescent in letting out some of the tension associated with them. Exercise (such as hiking, kickboxing, basketball, etc.), journaling, baking, or cooking are some healthy pastimes for decompressing. Developing a new pastime can also help people relax and reduce stress. When you're taking on a new endeavor, like trying to stay upright on ice skates, sculpting

clay on a potter's wheel, or remaining afloat on a paddle board, it's hard to concentrate on issues and fears.

7. Set an example. Show kids how to handle their troublesome adolescent emotions rather than just telling them. Be a good role model for your partner, your friends, and the rest of your family. Allow your adolescent to observe how you handle problems, and let tact be your guide. Try casually noting, "I'm going for a run to help me relax" if you prefer to go for a run when you're stressed, rather than suggesting, "You should go running; it will really get you out of that horrible attitude."

8. When to Seek Assistance Sometimes a mental health issue is misunderstood as regular teenage angst. A sudden difficulty with academics, abrupt changes in sleep habits, self-destructive conduct (skipping class, drinking, taking undue risks, etc.),

and a fixation with death are some of the warning indicators, according to experts. Contact your school counselor for help and services if you think your adolescent may be going through a problem that goes beyond a temporary developmental stage. You should immediately get in touch with your local emergency services if you have any worries about your child's immediate safety.

9. Think about switching to an online high school. Parenting teenagers occasionally requires a strategic approach. Bullying, a need for fewer distractions, or a desire for a new group of pals might be the cause of your irate teen's feelings. The best way to give them a fresh start and improve their bad teen sentiments may be to enroll them in a virtual high school like Connections Academy. Discover how the advantages of online high school may aid struggling teenagers.

For parents, middle and high school years can be challenging for kids, but by implementing some of these best practices into your interactions, you can make this time less stressful.

Your teen will be better prepared for success in school and in life if you assist them in developing social and emotional skills for their general well-being. These include learning coping mechanisms; controlling emotions through being grateful; and changing one's perspective to focus on what they can control. Take a look at these six suggestions to enhance your student's social and emotional .

www.ingramcontent.com/pod-product-compliance
Lightning Source LLC
LaVergne TN
LVHW020533160826
845677LV00015B/4036

* 9 7 9 8 3 5 1 7 8 2 5 4 6 *